Josephine G. Cochran: *industrial dishwasher*

Sarah E. Ball: *combined work table and basket*

Maria E. Allen: *diaper*

Anna Connelly: *fire escape*

Anna Breadin: *school desk*

1890s

Margaret A. Wilcox: *car heater*

Annie Chilton: *house detacher*

Harriet R. Tracy: *"lock and chain" stitch for sewing machine*

Cynthia Westover: *street-cleaning cart*

Leonie Callmeyer: *means for detecting the opening of sealed envelopes*

Anna Mangin: *pastry fork*

Letitia Geer: *medical syringes*

1900s

Olivia Poole: *Jolly Jumper*

Elizabeth J. (Magie) Phillips: *The Landlord's Game (early version of Monopoly)*

Florence Parpart: *modern electric refrigerator*

Alice Parker: *gas-powered central heating*

Madeline Turner: *Turner's Fruit Press*

Mary Anderson: *windshield wiper*

Anonymous: *ice cream cone*

Catherine Ryan: *nut and bolt lock for railroad tracks*

Madam C. J. Walker: *hair-care products*

Melitta Bentz: *drip coffee machine*

Carrie B. Averill: *baby carrier*

Rose O'Neill: *Kewpie doll*

Mary P. Jacobs: *brassiere*

Laura M. Hicks: *wash mitt*

Madeline Turner: *fruit press*

May Conner: *combined egg beater and potato masher*

Ida Forbes: *electric hot water heater*

Julie Auerbach: *detachable, self-adjusting corset strap*

Marjorie Stewart Joyner: *permanent wave machine*

1930s

Ida Hyde: *microelectrode*

Beulah Louise Henry: *bobbin-free sewing machine; vacuum ice cream freezer (plus many others)*

Ruth Wakefield: *chocolate chip cookie*

Katherine Burr Blodgett: *nonreflecting glass ("invisible" glass)*

Gladys Whitcomb Geissmann: *glove construction*

1940s

Dr. Maria Telkes: *residential solar heating*

Angela Ruiz Robles: *Mechanical Encyclopedia (electronic book reader)*

Sonjade Lennart: *capri pants*

Hedwig Kiesler Maukey (also known as movie star Hedy Lamarr) (and George Antheil): *secret communication system using "frequency hopping"*

Henrietta Mahim Bradberry: *bed rack to freshen clothes*

Dorothy Rodgers: *Jonny Mop*

Alice King Chatham: *helmet used by Chuck Yeager when he broke the sound barrier*

Rachel Brown and Elizabeth Hazen: *Nystatin (antibiotic drug)*

1950s

Mary Sherman Morgan: *rocket fuel, Hydyne*

Bessie Blount Griffin: *electronic feeding device*

Ruth Benerito: *wash-and-wear cotton fabrics*

Anna Kalso: *earth shoes*

Rosalyn Yalow: *radioimmunoassay (medical tool)*

Marion Donovan: *disposable diaper*

Grace Murray Hopper: *computer compiler*

Virginia Apgar: *Apgar score*

Gertrude Elion: *wonder drugs for treatment of leukemia and kidney transplant rejection*

Patsy O. Sherman: *Scotchgard*

Bette Nesmith Graham: *Liquid Paper*

Ruth Handler: *Barbie doll*

1960s

Marie Van Brittan Brown: *CCTV*

Yvonne Brill: *space rocket propulsion system*

Teresa and Mary Thompson (eight and nine years old): *solar teepee*

Ann Moore: *Snugli baby carrier*

Mary Davidson Kenner: *carrier attachment for walking aid*

Betty Galloway (ten years old): *bubble-making toy*

Pansy Ellen Essman: *Pansey-ette bath aid (sponge pillow to keep babies secure in the bath)*

1970s

Shirley Ann Jackson: *telecommunications foundations*

Ingeborg Hochmair (co-inventor): *modern cochlear implant*

Stephanie Kwolek: *Kevlar*

Erna Schneider Hoover: *telephone switching system*

Becky Schroeder: *Glo-sheet*

Barbara Askins: *Autoradiograph (photographic technique for NASA)*

Virgie M. Amnions: *fireplace damper actuating tool*

Ruth Siems: *instant stuffing mix*

1980s

Dr. Patricia Bath: *Laserphaco Probe*

Flossie Wong-Staal: *cloning and expression of HIV-1 DNA*

Randi Altschul: *various toys*

Rachel Zimmerman Brachman: *Blissymbol printer*

Radia Perlman: *spanning-tree protocol (STP)*

Magdalena Villaruz: *turtle-powered hand tractor*

Ellen Ochoa: *optical systems for space*

Olga D. Gonzalez-Sanabria: *battery separator for alkaline battery*

TIMELINE CONTINUES AT END OF BOOK.

Girls Think of EVERYTHING

Stories of INGENIOUS INVENTIONS by Women

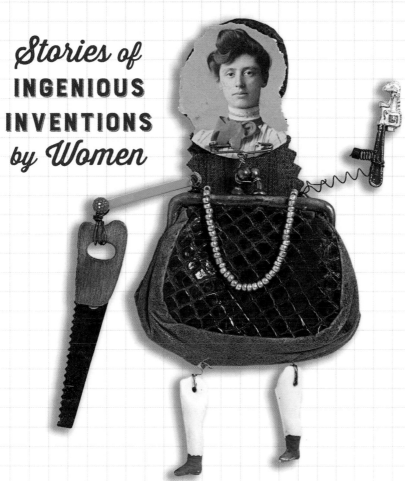

Catherine Thimmesh

ILLUSTRATED BY Melissa Sweet

HOUGHTON MIFFLIN HARCOURT
Boston   New York

hmhco.com

Kevlar® is a registered trademark of Du Pont.
Scotchgard™ is a trademark of 3M.
Snugli® is a registered trademark of Snugli, Incorporated.
LuminAID® is a registered trademark of LuminAID.
Roominate® is a registered trademark of Roominate, LLC.

The text of this book is set in 14-point Fairfield.
The illustrations are mixed media.
Collages photographed by Hugh Brantner Photography

The Library of Congress has cataloged the hardcover edition as follows:
Thimmesh, Catherine.
Girls think of everything: stories of ingenious inventions by women / by Catherine Thimmesh;
illustrated by Melissa Sweet.
p. cm.
Summary: Tells the story of how women throughout the ages have responded to situations confronting
them in daily life by inventing such items as solar lanterns, baby carriers, and space bumpers.
RNF ISBN 0-395-93744-2 PAP ISBN 0-618-19563-7.
1. Women inventors—United States—Biography—Juvenile literature. 2. Inventions—United States—
History—Juvenile literature. [1. Inventors. 2. Inventions. 3. Women Biography.] I. Sweet, Melissa, ill. II.
Title
T39.T48 2000
609.2'273—dc2I [B] 99-36270 CIP

ISBN: 978-1-328-77253-4 paper over board

Manufactured in China
SCP 10 9 8 7 6 5 4 3 2 1
4500715768

For Jaimie and Simon, who invent new ways
to amuse me every day
—C.T.

In memory of Jamien Morehouse, who
invented many wonderful things
—M.S.

INVENTION STORIES

IN THE BEGINNING . . .

With a push you are free—bursting into the world scrunched up and screaming. "It's a girl!" the doctor announces. Or "It's a boy!" And so your life began. And with those very first breaths, and in those very first moments, your health and well-being were evaluated through the eyes of an ingenious inventor: Dr. Virginia Apgar. Dr. Apgar developed the Newborn Scoring System—or Apgar score—to measure five crucial aspects of a baby's health: color, pulse, reflexes, activity, and respiration. She recognized the urgency of identifying those newborns in need of emergency attention, and because of her innovation, hundreds of thousands of lives have been saved. Today, all medical professionals evaluate a new baby using the Apgar Score within minutes of birth. Right from the get-go, a woman's inventiveness and ingenuity touched your life. But that was only the beginning.

Whether in medicine or science, household products or high-tech gadgets, women and girls invent—and their inventions surround us and affect our everyday lives. They have created cancer-fighting drugs, space bumpers, coffeemakers, and sleeping-bag coats to warm the homeless. Women have invented games and toys and computer software programs.

"At first people refuse to believe that a strange new thing can be done, then they begin to hope it can be done, then they see it can be done—then it is done and all the world wonders why it was not done centuries ago."
—Frances Hodgson Burnett, author of *The Secret Garden*

Inventors create for a variety of reasons. Maybe you've heard the saying "Necessity is the mother of invention"? It's true. An inventor sees a need and seeks to fill it. A long time ago, before there were record keepers or materials to keep records on, people went about their daily lives. And in doing so, they invented. According to oral tradition, as well as observations and studies conducted by anthropologists, women were responsible for some of the most fundamental and enduring innovations of all time. Because of their responsibilities within their families and communities, it appears that women were the first to invent tools and utensils—including the mortar (a heavy bowl) and pestle (a clublike hammer) to prepare food, such as flour, and botanical medicines.

They spun cotton together with flax, thereby inventing cloth. And they created the first shelters by designing and constructing huts and wigwams. It is said that women were the first to discover dyes to color cloth and tanning methods to make leather goods.

Throughout history, women have always been innovators. But their accomplishments have often been downplayed, skimmed over, or ignored altogether. In the year 1715, we have the first documented evidence of an invention by an American woman. Sybilla Masters invented a power-driven method for cleaning and curing corn based on her observations of Native American women using heavy pestles to pound the corn by hand.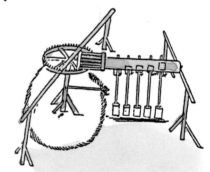

Unfortunately, at that time, women were not allowed patents in their own names. In fact, women did not legally own any property whatsoever and were themselves considered to be the property of their husbands. So, for Sybilla to protect her invention, she had to settle for obtaining the patent in the name of her husband, Thomas Masters.

Nearly one hundred years would pass before an American woman's invention would legally be recognized as her own. Mary Dixon Kies has the honor of holding the first U.S. patent ever awarded to a woman in her own name. Mary created an innovative process of weaving straw with silk or thread, primarily for use in ladies' bonnets. She was awarded a patent in 1809, just as straw bonnets were becoming extremely fashionable.

Against the odds, women have invented. They succeeded when many thought they'd fail. Madam C. J. Walker, the daughter of former slaves, invented hair-care products for African American women and a new method for selling them. She was born Sarah Breedlove, was orphaned at the age of seven, married at fourteen, and widowed at twenty. For nearly twenty years she labored doing other people's laundry. Madam Walker began her business with a single product, a lot of confidence, and a dollar fifty. She went door-to-door giving free demonstrations and showing before-and-after photos of herself. Within seven years, she had several hair-care products and a thriving business. Madam C. J. Walker went on to become the first American woman self-made millionaire.

These days, door-to-door demonstrations have been replaced with website tutorials and Internet crowdfunding campaigns and reality television shows. One-to-one

Many inventions evolve out of general curiosity—a sense of interest, a sense of "Wouldn't it be fun if . . . ?" And nothing says fun quite like a superhero arm . . . that shoots sparkly glitter. When she was just ten years old and away at camp, Jordan Reeves—who was born without her left forearm—used a 3D printer to invent her own unique prosthetic arm that shoots a blast of shiny sparkles. Because, why not? "You can never be sad with sparkles," she says.

salesmanship has given way to one-to-millions-of-viewers-at-a-time pitch fests. Lori Greiner, like Madam Walker, began with a single product—a jewelry organizer—which she was able to pitch on TV (on the QVC home shopping network) and quickly went on to sell half a million organizers. And that was only the beginning. Lori has since amassed more than 120 patents of her own, a business empire, and has helped other inventors—especially other women—successfully launch more than 450 different products!

But of course it isn't just Americans who are innovators. All around the globe—from Italy to India, from Nova Scotia to New Zealand—women and girls invent.

In the Askar refugee camp in the West Bank, three Palestinian girls invented an electronic walking stick for the blind, and they went on to win a special award in electronics at the prestigious Intel Science and Engineering Fair in 2010. Nour Al-Ardah, Aseel Sha'ar, and Aseel Abu Leil, guided by their supervisor, Jameelah Khaled, created an electronic sensor cane that sends infrared signals both frontward *and* downward—solving a fundamental flaw of previous electronic canes—by detecting not only the obstacles in front, but simultaneously the holes and pitfalls in the ground below.

Today, in living rooms and labs, women and girls are inventing. They are combining their curiosity and creativity with persistence and optimism. They are imagining. They are thinking and talking. "What if . . . ?" they ask. "How about . . . ?" they wonder. "Aha!" they exclaim.

And gradually their ingenuity emerges: an inventiveness that touches all our lives, and perhaps energizes our own creativity—women and men, girls and boys alike. These are a few of their stories.

RUTH WAKEFIELD
Chocolate Chip Cookies

The horses were tired; they were hungry. Time to grab a bite on the journey from Boston to New Bedford: a little hay, maybe some oats. After all, the busy Toll House on Route 18 in Whitman, Massachusetts, was a rest stop for horses. But in time, that would all change. Hay and oats would give way to salads and soups and chicken in white sauce. And, as luck would have it, chocolate chip cookies.

It was an accident. A simple mistake. A last-minute effort to save time. A just-toss-it-in-and-it-will-all-work-out sort of gesture . . . but it led to Ruth Wakefield's creation of the crunchy, chewy, oh-so-delicious chocolate chip cookie. Her invention is one of the most enduring, one of the most duplicated, and one of the most loved creations ever.

Ruth's restaurant was relatively new. She and her husband had taken the old Toll House and converted it into a dining establishment—the Toll House Inn—serving people this time, not horses. Early on, it was small, with space to seat thirty. As co-owner, manager, hostess, and cook, Ruth kept very busy. One day in 1930, she was making a batch of chocolate butter drop cookies, popular at the time. The recipe required her to melt chocolate squares and pour the chocolate into the batter before baking.

Instead, because she was in a hurry, she simply broke the chocolate into chunks and tossed them in the mix, figuring they would melt when the cookies baked. She figured wrong. She stared in amazement at her pan of ruined chocolate butter drops: cookies speckled with chunks of chocolate. But then Ruth tasted them. And so did her customers. The result? Undeniably delicious.

As the restaurant grew in popularity, Ruth's Toll House cookies quickly became famous. At the Nestlé candy company,

Enough chocolate chips cookies are baked each year to circle the globe 10 times.

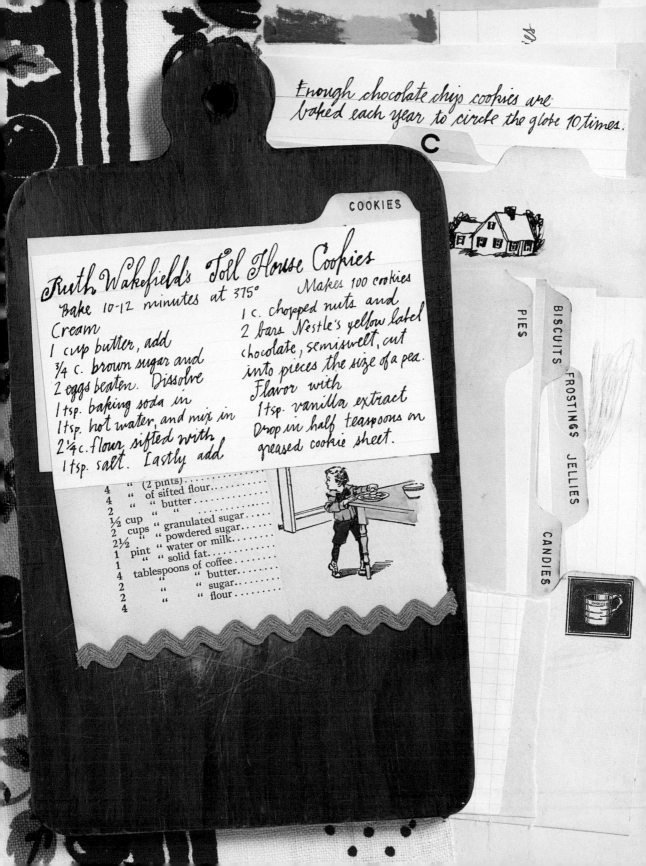

Ruth Wakefield's Toll House Cookies

Bake 10-12 minutes at 375°   Makes 100 cookies

Cream
1 cup butter, add
3/4 c. brown sugar and
2 eggs beaten. Dissolve
1 tsp. baking soda in
1 tsp. hot water, and mix in
2 1/4 c. flour sifted with
1 tsp. salt. Lastly add

1 c. chopped nuts and
2 bars Nestle's yellow label
chocolate, semisweet, cut
into pieces the size of a pea.
Flavor with
1 tsp. vanilla extract
Drop in half teaspoons on
greased cookie sheet.

4 " (2 pints)		
4 " of sifted flour		
2 " " butter		
1/2 cup "		
2 cups " granulated sugar		
2 1/2 " powdered sugar		
1 pint " water or milk		
1 " solid fat		
4 tablespoons of coffee		
2 " " butter		
2 " " sugar		
4 " " flour		

curious sales managers set out to investigate their sudden jump in sales of chocolate bars in the eastern region. They quickly located the source: Ruth Wakefield.

At Ruth's request, Nestlé agreed to score, or cut lines in, their chocolate bars to make them easier to break. Several years later, in 1939, Nestlé decided they could make it easier still. They created the chocolate morsel, or chip, specifically for use in Ruth Wakefield's cookies. They even bought the rights to the Toll House name and, with Ruth's permission, published her recipe right on the back of their chocolate chip package. In exchange, Ruth reportedly was given a lifetime's worth of free chocolate. Today, her invention is still wildly popular. There are countless chocolate chip cookie variations floating around, and new ones pop up regularly. Lots of people are becoming rather creative with their cookies. Some are even adding oats.

> Today's multimillion-dollar chocolate chip industry is a direct result of Ruth's chocolate melting mistake. Nearly one hundred million bags of chocolate chips are sold every year. That's enough to make five billion cookies a year, or fourteen million cookies a day.

ANNA STORK AND ANDREA SRESHTA

Lumin AID

It's dark outside. Not a light in sight. No flickers of brightness seeping through windows. No streetlights aglow. Certainly no neon signs blinking a city's hello. Just a deep, dark, velvety black—a hallmark of the wilderness . . . or a widespread power outage.

It was in 1879 that Thomas Edison invented the first practical electric light bulb. Over a hundred years later, in 2010, Anna Stork and Andrea Sreshta invented an ingenious lantern for when the lights go out.

Andrea and Anna were graduate students at Columbia University when a devastating earthquake struck Haiti in January of 2010—killing more than 200,000 people and leaving nearly 2 million displaced and homeless.

Both students were drawn to enroll in a studio class (working on independent projects) that revolved around designing disaster relief aid. The horrific images coming out of Haiti drove home the idea that a successful project could have a real-world impact.

"One of the things that really struck us," says Anna, *"was the extremely high incidence of things like kidnapping, violent assault, and theft—and how dangerous it was for these people living in these tents, basically living on top of each other."*

So Anna and Andrea focused their attention on how to improve the living space and the day-to-day living experience for all those people who had lost everything, and on top of that, now faced a life of danger.

In the brainstorming phase, they explored different aspects of water filtration, but very quickly turned their attention to lighting instead. It was a need that had not been met, and they felt fulfilling that need could genuinely and substantially improve the horrific conditions so many people in disaster situations faced.

"We zeroed in on a floatable, solar, rechargeable light pretty

quickly," explains Anna. "But finding the right type of solar panels, the right size solar panels, and the right type of battery, and really balancing the performance parameters took a lot of iterating."

They also experimented with different plastic materials for the outer casing. They had three must-meet criteria: the solar light must be completely waterproof (it had to work in flooding situations, or out in the rain); it had to be durable, because a punctured light is a broken light; and it needed to be lightweight and convenient to carry.

The LuminAID lanterns need between seven and ten hours of sunlight to fully charge. A fully charged lantern provides thirty hours of light—enough for five evenings, providing six hours of light each night.

"So the whole idea—the foundation of this idea—was that it would be easily distributed in times of emergency, and also easy for people to carry around and charge on the go," explains Anna. "We also wanted it to pack flat, which meant it needed to be inflatable."

Anna and Andrea spent the semester prototyping: trying different plastics, inflatable valves, batteries, solar panels, and LEDs. (The very first prototype consisted of a small ziplock plastic bag, a sports bottle cap as a valve for inflating, tissue paper to diffuse light, and a simple solar circuit taped on the inside.) They also developed a business plan that included selling to individuals for outdoor use.

To raise money for professional prototyping and manufacturing, they mounted a crowdfunding campaign on Indiegogo—an Internet site where people can pledge money to a project in exchange for rewards, usually the product itself. It quickly became clear how interested people were in the product for personal uses—camping, outdoor parties, emergency supplies—and also how inspired they were in the relief mission through a "Give Light, Get Light" offer. After the Indiegogo campaign, they started selling the lanterns (in 2011) via their website.

And then, after a lengthy application and audition process, Andrea and Anna pitched LuminAID on *Shark Tank*—a hit reality TV show on which five highly successful business people (the "sharks") hear pitches from aspiring entrepreneurs and decide whether or not to invest their money and expertise in the people and their products.

"We got five offers—one from each of the sharks," says Anna. *"And the thing about* Shark Tank *is that it keeps re-airing, and on multiple channels, so that whole year just kept going up in terms of our sales and the publicity we were getting. It was really, really exciting!"*

The LuminAID business continues to grow—distributing

LuminAID offers a variety of different lanterns at different prices. In 2017, they released a lantern that also charges a cell phone! And in just a few short years of business, they have distributed tens of thousands of lights to disaster victims, including those affected by Hurricane Isaac in Haiti, Typhoon Haiyan in the Philippines, and an earthquake in Nepal (distributed through their partner relief organizations).

lights through NGO relief organizations, selling to customers online, selling to retailers to stock on store shelves, providing custom brand printing, and shipping to more than sixty countries around the globe.

Now, in the deep, dark, velvety black, an innovative lantern will help a child do his homework in a tent; a hiker off exploring can find her way out of the woods; and a family—in the aftermath of disaster—can maintain a sense of comfort and safety night after night.

MARY ANDERSON
Windshield Wipers

It was a dreadful day, weather-wise. Snow and sleet pelted the pavement, and people burrowed deep within their coats. Hoping to catch the sights and escape the blustery cold, Mary Anderson of Birmingham, Alabama, climbed aboard a New York City streetcar. The year was 1902. It turned out to be a ride she would never forget, but not because of the scenery. Instead, the ride would inspire her to invent the very first windshield wiper. And simply because she felt sorry for the streetcar driver, who struggled to see through the glass. The invention not only would improve conditions for all drivers, but would save countless lives as well.

Earlier, top-notch engineers had tackled the problem of poor visibility in bad weather and came up with a solution. They split the windshield. Once the glass became covered with rain or snow, the streetcar driver could fling open the middle for a clear view. Trouble was, it didn't work. At least, not very well. Mary watched helplessly as the driver desperately tried to see. When he opened the split glass, he was greeted with a burst of icy-cold air and a blast of heavy, wet snow.

"Why doesn't someone create a device to remove the snow?" Mary reportedly asked the people around her.

"It's been tried many times," they told her. *"Can't be done."*

Nonsense, thought Mary, as she scribbled in her notebook. Why can't there be a lever on the inside that would move an arm on the outside to swipe off the snow? To her, it seemed perfectly simple.

Before windshield wipers were widely available, drivers used to smear pieces of carrots or onions across the glass to create an oily film that they hoped would repel water.

Later, when she returned to her home in Birmingham, she studied her sketches. She spent some time refining her drawings—making them more elaborate, adding more details. Satisfied at last, she brought her design to a

small manufacturing company in Birmingham and hired them to make a model. Then, she filed a patent application.

"My invention relates to an improvement in window-cleaning devices in which a radially-swinging arm is actuated by a handle from inside of a car-vestibule," Mary stated in her patent specification.

In other words, a lever on the inside that would move an arm on the outside. Mary's wiper was made of wooden strips and pieces of rubber. She designed it to be removed in good weather so that it would not interfere with the appearance of the streetcar. One of her most important elements was the addition of a counterweight.

"This was used," she wrote, *"to provide means for maintaining a uniform pressure upon the glass throughout the entire area swept by my improved window-cleaning device."*

In other words, it would swipe off the snow. Mary was awarded a patent in 1903 for a window-cleaning device—a windshield wiper. Once the invention was protected by patent, she wrote a large Canadian company offering to sell her rights. They weren't interested. After reviewing her proposal, they decided that her invention had little, if any, commercial value. They simply didn't think it would sell. They encouraged her, however, to submit any other "useful patents" she might have for their consideration.

Mary put the patent in a drawer and, eventually, it expired. Several years later, someone else revived her idea, patented it, sold it, and made a very large sum of money. Every day, lives are saved due to increased visibility during bad weather. Even in our high-tech society, the windshield wiper remains one of the greatest safety inventions of the modern-day automobile. And tourists can now see the sights despite the snow, sleet, or rain.

AZZA ABDELHAMID FAIAD

Turning Plastic into Fuel

The cars of the future are just around the bend. They'll fly! They'll float! They'll drive themselves! They'll be fueled by plastic!

Fueling a car (or bus or boat or plane) with discarded plastic bags and soda bottles sounds preposterous to most people. But Azza Faiad is not most people.

As a teenager living in Alexandria, Egypt, Azza was very interested in science competitions and the corresponding challenges they presented. In ninth grade, she began researching the winning projects from the prestigious Intel International Engineering and Science Fair, becoming more and more inspired to undertake her own project.

"My life was kind of boring," Azza says. "I was the kind of student who just keeps studying, and that was not really fun. So I wanted to do something that I enjoyed and that I might also use for my future."

Azza was drawn to some pressing real-world problems—specifically, eliminating plastic waste (well over a million tons per year in Egypt alone and thirty-three million tons in the United States—none of it biodegradable). Millions of fish, birds, and marine mammals die from plastic waste each year—and those numbers are increasing.

She also wanted to ease some of the strains of the energy crisis—brought into stark relief for Azza when a refueling stop took over an hour of waiting in line.

"So I came to the conclusion that I should be tackling these two problems and coming up with a solution to both of them," explains Azza. "So I thought, why not reuse this waste as a source of energy?"

It wasn't a novel idea; others have tried—and some have succeeded in turning plastics into fuel. But what makes Azza's invention unique was her use of a never-before-used catalyst to accelerate the chemical reaction necessary to break down the plastic. (A catalyst speeds up a chemical reaction, while

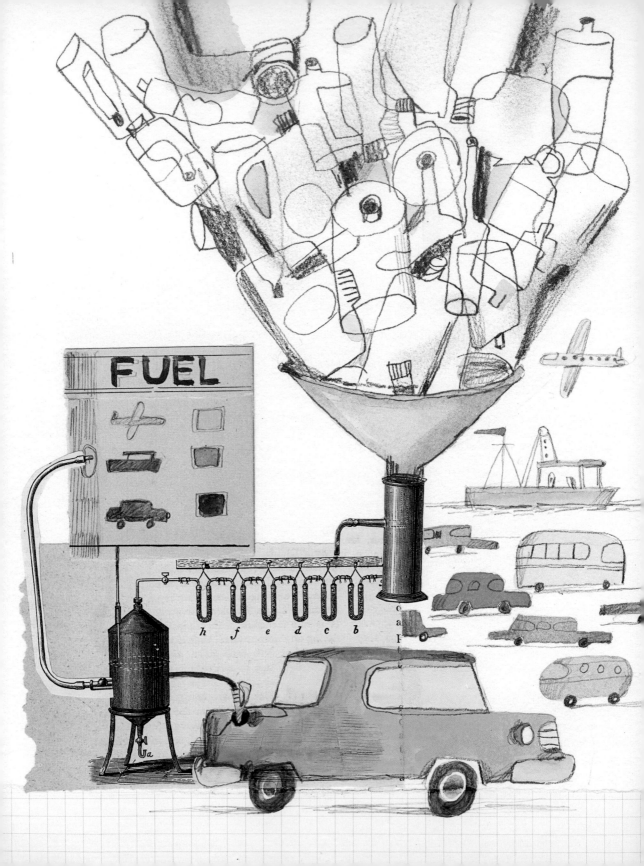

its own chemical composition remains unchanged—not becoming part of the reaction or the product.) And what makes Azza's invention even more tantalizing is its low, low cost.

> Azza estimates that a million tons of plastic waste could generate $163 million worth of fuel substance—in addition to the untold benefits of ridding the planet of the excessive plastic choking landfills and waters.

"It took me a while to actually understand all the chemistry behind it," Azza confesses. *"I had two mentors and they were really the most helpful in the process because I didn't have much experience."*

Azza spent months researching and experimenting, experimenting and researching, and still experimenting. She left her family to travel to Cairo (about two hours from her hometown) to conduct experiments in a state-of-the-art lab with a team of skilled scientists at the Petroleum Institute of Egypt.

One particular catalyst from the research had proven to be the best at cracking and breaking down the plastic—but it was extremely expensive, which meant implementing the process on a large scale would be too pricey. Azza's idea was to search out a catalyst with a very similar chemical composition to the proven (but expensive) catalyst until she found one that would also be low cost.

"So we ran three types of catalysts and were running the same experiments with them," she explains. *"Two of them were mentioned widely in the research, and the third was this new calcium-based catalyst. We wanted to see the different spectrum of results."*

The experiments showed that the calcium-based catalyst of Azza's hypothesis not only succeeded in cracking and breaking down the plastic (a process known as catalytic cracking—which produces both gaseous and liquid byproducts), but it worked more efficiently and under lower temperatures (making it potentially safer). The liquid byproducts would become feedstock for gasoline, to fuel the likes of cars and buses; while the gaseous byproducts could be used for natural gas, to heat homes, for example.

And to add to the success, Azza's calcium-based catalyst was low cost, easy to obtain, and easy to ship—thus making it rise above the others.

"My science project was not about reinventing energy," explains Azza. *"It was about making this energy cheaper and more efficient."*

Not to mention helping the environment along the way.

Azza's goal is to develop a sound business plan for a sustainable waste management system—particularly for developing countries like Egypt—and put her plastics-to-fuel invention to commercial use.

Which seems like a good idea since it appears the future is no longer around the bend, but is actually on the horizon. Already companies are testing flying cars and self-driving cars (self-driving cars are expected to be in widespread use by the mid-2020s). And so it wouldn't be surprising at all if one day we saw cars powered by the ideas of an enterprising teenager coupled with a big old pile of plastic waste.

At a science fair, a male competitor made disparaging comments about her headscarf. Azza says she realized, "I am not here just to win an award. I am here to change the world's view of women and girls in developing countries—particularly Muslim girls in a scientific community."

STEPHANIE KWOLEK

Kevlar

Skillfully gliding down the snow-packed mountain, a skier is unaware of an amazing material improving the performance of her skis. It is a mysterious material found also in airplanes and athletic shoes. In tires and ropes and gloves. In boats, boots, and bullet-resistant vests.

It's strong—incredibly strong—bullet-stopping strong. It is also flexible and incredibly light—it can shave eight hundred pounds off an aircraft frame. A material that was once a mere fiction, found only in Superman's suit, is now a

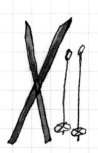

fact. Thanks to Stephanie Kwolek, inventor of Kevlar, we now have a fiber that is five times stronger than steel and used in everything from skis and sailboats to space vehicles. As a research chemist for the Du Pont company, Stephanie was assigned to find the next generation of high-performance fiber.

"At that time, we had heard that there was the potential for a petroleum shortage," explains Stephanie. "We were thinking that if we could get a very strong and very stiff, lightweight fiber, then we could use it to reinforce radial tires. This would make the tires lighter, and therefore you would use less energy because the vehicle would be lighter."

Stephanie spent a few months experimenting with very stiff chain polymers. (A polymer is a chemical compound made up of repeating structural units.) One day she prepared an unusual solution. When she stirred the solution, it turned opalescent—or pearl-like. When she put some on a spatula and let

Kevlar saves lives. Since Du Pont began documenting survivors in 1987, more than 3,100 police officers have been saved by wearing bullet-resistant Kevlar vests. Firefighters are protected with comfortable Kevlar boots that are able to withstand extreme heat and resist sharp objects.

KEVLAR®

LIGHTER THAN NYLON

STIFFER THAN FIBERGLASS

POLYESTER CAN MELT, KEVLAR IS NON-MELTING

MORE DURABLE THAN LEATHER

STRONGER THAN STEEL

MORE THERMAL STABILITY THAN ASBESTOS

it flow down freely, it was cohesive, like glue. It was also very thin, like water. Amazingly, it was a liquid crystalline solution—part liquid, part solid. Stephanie immediately thought that Du Pont could spin the solution into fiber. But when she took it to a technician, he refused to put it in the spinning apparatus, claiming that the cloudiness and texture of the solution meant there were still bits of solid particles in it—material that would clog the tiny holes of the spinneret.

"I went back to the laboratory, and I thought, well, maybe he does have a point," Stephanie says. *"So I filtered it and I found that when the solution passed through a fine-pore glass funnel, it was just as cloudy on the other side, so I knew it didn't have solid material in it."*

Stephanie talked to the technician on and off for a couple of weeks, gently prodding and persuading him to spin her solution. Finally, he agreed. Once the fibers were made, she sent them to the physical-testing lab to determine its properties, such as strength and stiffness. The results were astonishing. She had the fibers tested again. And again.

Once, NASA used a twelve-mile Kevlar cable—thinner than a pencil—to secure a 1,200-pound satellite during a space shuttle mission.

"When I got the numbers back, I was rather skeptical," she recalls. "I thought maybe they'd made a mistake—and I certainly didn't want to embarrass myself by telling anyone."

As it turned out, Stephanie didn't embarrass herself. She had invented a remarkable technology and, as a result, a fiber that would forever change the field of polymer chemistry and make many millions of dollars for Du Pont. She was rewarded with a generous bonus and a long-overdue promotion. Many people came on board during the development phase, and Stephanie is quick to point out that some of them made very significant contributions to the final product. There was a tremendous amount of excitement in the lab—as well as secrecy. And were there any problems?

As a young girl, Stephanie loved making elaborate paper doll outfits. She would also make outfits from cloth—sneaking in time on her mom's sewing machine. Early on, she had her future career narrowed down to two things: scientist or fashion designer. With the invention of Kevlar, Stephanie got to be both.

"There were millions!" says Stephanie, laughing. "Many times we almost gave up because it was such a contrary fiber. And of course before

you can commercialize something, the whole process and product have to be very reliable."

Every step was a challenge, she says. Every step a learning process. In 1971, Kevlar fiber was spun in the Du Pont plant for the first time. Today, all you need to do is look around. Kevlar is everywhere. It is used in hundreds of products, including sailboats, rackets, and racing cars. In downhill skis, woven layers of Kevlar reduce weight and lessen vibration. In athletic shoes, it gives stronger and more flexible foot support and disperses shock. In fact, the product can be used whenever and wherever a very strong, very stiff, lightweight fiber is needed. Any ideas?

ALISSA CHAVEZ
Hot Seat

People forget. It happens. Usually, the forgetfulness is merely inconvenient—misplaced keys, or forgotten homework. But sometimes—sometimes—a moment of forgetfulness can suddenly bring life to a devastating halt.

Every year, roughly forty-two children (mostly under the age of two) die in hot cars because they've been accidentally forgotten in the back seat (usually because they're quietly sound asleep). If it's eighty degrees outside, it takes just ten minutes for the interior of a car to reach a blistering ninety-nine degrees and a body to quickly overheat, causing heatstroke.

Alissa Chavez, a young teenager in Albuquerque, was heartbroken reading of three such incidents that happened in one year alone in and around Albuquerque. She took it upon herself to actually do something about it and invented the Hot Seat, which alerts parents and saves the lives of children.

"With all the technology and the things we have out there," says Alissa, "I just thought there had to be a way to prevent something like that from happening. And so, for my eighth grade science project I did research about these horrible statistics and it made me want to do something to prevent it."

Her invention won numerous awards at the science fair and also received a lot of positive feedback. She decided to bring the idea beyond a school project, turn it into an actual product, and help save young lives as often as possible.

Her first prototype (the one exhibited at the science fair) was a visual alarm from RadioShack that she positioned in the car toward the car seat. She had a doll in the car seat, and whenever the camera detected the doll, the alarm would go off. The alarm was also connected to a key fob, so if the parent walked off, the key fob would sound the alarm as well.

Needing money to further develop the idea and create professional, working prototypes, she turned to the crowdfunding source Indiegogo. Alissa was skeptical that it would work—she needed to raise thousands of dollars.

"It turned out I was really lucky," says Alissa, *"because when I started my crowdfunding campaign, I got an award from the mayor of Albuquerque for my invention. And the media was there . . . and people heard about it and donated to my campaign."*

One of the rewards of winning the science fair was to have lunch with the mayor and present her invention. A few years later, when Alissa had the first real prototype, she took it upon herself to call the mayor's office and update him. He invited her to come and meet with his staff to discuss prototyping and small businesses. He also surprised her with an award at a press conference with the media present. The media coverage of Alissa's award and invention drove traffic to her crowdfunding campaign—a very happy coincidence.

After experimenting with several designs—mostly a trial-and-error process—she settled on the fifth prototype. By this time, the Hot Seat product had morphed into a small pouch—more of a sensor pad—that was placed under the padding of a car seat, with weight sensors to detect the presence of a child, and then linked via Bluetooth to a smartphone app.

If the caregiver moves more than fifteen to twenty feet away from the car, and the sensor in the pouch detects a child, an alarm on the app will go off, alerting the caregiver to the child left behind.

"I hired a team of engineers," Alissa explains. "And we worked together on all of that—on trying the different sensors, the different batteries—even the circuit board changed a ton of times. It was really cool to actually see my idea coming to life in front of me."

It was a difficult process because it had never been done before and they ran into all kinds of problems that hadn't been solved yet, such as lengthy battery life, getting the sensors to communicate to the app, keeping the radius on Bluetooth a constant (so the alarm would trigger at a given distance), keeping the circuit board (and batteries) thin enough so the pad would remain thin and comfortable enough to place in the car seat.

Alissa Chavez is thought to be the youngest Latina woman to have received a U.S. patent (as of 2017). She applied for a patent when she was just fourteen years old, and was issued patent number 9,000,906 in April 2015, when she was seventeen years old!

But despite the problems, Alissa now has a product, she has several patents, and she's ready to make a difference—despite her young age.

"Well, innovation is what we need, right?" Alissa says. "And I think that comes from all ages. I think we all have a different perspective and that allows us to create amazing products."

With Alissa's invention of the Hot Seat, a moment of forgetfulness doesn't have to turn into a tragedy—and, consequently, the safety and care of our children has taken a giant leap forward.

GRACE MURRAY HOPPER
Computer Compiler

No one thought it was possible. Giving a computer commands in English—using words rather than mathematical code—was said to be a ridiculous idea. And creating a method that allowed for automatic programming was also considered laughable. But for mathematician and navy officer Grace Murray Hopper, such ideas were not only logical, but also necessary and inevitable. When Grace created the first computer compilers, she paved the way for computer programming as we know it today. The high-level computer languages that run our banks, our businesses, and our government have been developed by drawing upon her innovations. Even computer games descend from her pioneering work in programming. For the first time, Grace's compilers allowed non-mathematicians to use computers for many different tasks both in business and for private use.

"No one thought of that earlier because they weren't as lazy as I was," Grace said. *"A lot of our programmers liked to play with the bits. I wanted to get jobs done. That's what the computer was there for."*

In the beginning, when computers were first being developed, Grace and her fellow mathematicians did the programming by using mathematical code—plugging in numbers as commands. A combination of zeros and ones would have a specific meaning. For example, if Grace wanted to stop the computer, she would enter "1001100." She had to enter every program individually—even when many of them shared several of the same steps. Not only was this method very time-consuming, but, as Grace pointed out, it was also extremely easy to make mistakes. One incorrect number could ruin the whole program.

"It was so obvious," stated Grace. *"Why start from scratch with every single program you write? Develop one that would do a lot of the basic work over and over again. Developing a compiler was a logical move."*

file

enter

start

0 1 0 1 1 0 1

1 1 0 0 1 0 1 0

DEBUGGING 0 1 0

MORLEY 5081

"BUT WE'VE ALWAYS DONE it THAT WAY." IN THE COMPUTER INDUSTRY, WITH CHANGES COMING AS FAST AS THEY DO, YOU JUST CAN'T AFFORD TO HAVE PEOPLE SAYING THAT.

Logical, that was, for Grace. For her colleagues and superiors at the Remington Rand Company, a computer compiler was considered undoable.

Grace kept a clock in her office that ran counterclockwise—or backwards. It was a daily reminder to herself and anyone who visited her office that things could, in fact, be done differently. According to Grace, the worst phrase in the English language is "But we've always done it that way."

Grace proved otherwise. In 1952, she developed the A-0 System—a program, or set of instructions, that could transform mathematical code into machine code. To do this, she plucked specific pieces of code from several programs and gave each piece an individual call number so she could locate it and arrange it in the order needed. She then combined the separate pieces of code onto magnetic tape.

"All I had to do was to write down a set of call numbers, let the computer find them on the tape, bring them over, and do the additions," explained Grace. "This was the first compiler. We could start writing mathematical equations and let the computer do the work."

With the success of her A-0 compiler, she moved ahead to develop the B-0 System, a compiler that could understand instructions given in English (later to be called FLOW-MATIC). Her new compiler, she explained, would act as a translator of sorts—converting letters of the alphabet into the recognizable language of machine code. Her goal? To create a user-friendly computer. Once again, Grace was told, "It can't be done." But once again, she did it anyway.

"When you have a good idea and you've tried it and you know it's going to work, go ahead and do it," she said, *"because it is much easier to apologize later than it is to get permission."*

By 1957, Grace's FLOW-MATIC was one of three computer programming languages used in American computers, and the only one that could understand English commands. It quickly became apparent, however, that a universal computer language

> In the summer of 1945, Grace and her colleagues were working on the enormous, fifty-foot-long IBM computer called the Mark II when suddenly the computer stopped. Upon investigation, they discovered that a moth had gotten in and caused a relay to fail. They carefully removed the moth and taped it in their logbook along with the notation "first actual case of a bug being found." From then on, when their supervisor asked why they weren't calculating faster, they told him they were busy "debugging" the computer. The term has been with us ever since.

was necessary—one language that could be used to run all computers. And Grace's position? Leading the movement for standardization. Without a single language, she insisted, the entire computer industry would be "dead in the water."

Grace Hopper's innovative compilers ultimately served as road maps for the development of COBOL (**co**mmon **b**usiness **o**riented **l**anguage), the first universal computer language to be used in government and business computers. And thanks to her user-friendly programming ideas, today's high-level programming languages were made possible. High-level languages, for example, that drive computer games. Now all you have to do is figure out how to win them.

TRISHA PRABHU
ReThink

Ping: *"Hey what's up?"*

   Ping: *"Homework. Ugh."*

   Messaging friends via text, IM, and social media is what adolescents and teens do.

Ping: *"You're such a jerk."*

Ping: *"Everyone hates you."*

Unfortunately, it's what cyberbullies do too.

But now, thanks to an innovative app created by Trisha Prabhu, there's an easy way for adolescents and teens to pause . . . to slow down and reconsider whether or not their words might be hurtful. Trisha's invention gives them a last-minute-before-it's-too-late chance to *ReThink* before they hit send.

Trisha was in eighth grade when she read an article about an eleven-year-old girl in Florida who was literally cyberbullied to her death. The young girl, Rebecca, took her own life after enduring relentless bullying for well over a year.

"That was something that was just shocking to me," Trisha recalls. *"I started looking into it and started researching what was really a very multifaceted issue. And it became evident to me that someone needed to step up—someone needed to take charge—and I decided I wanted to be the advocate; I wanted to be the person to do that."*

Trisha found brain development intriguing: how it develops from back to front; how 90 percent of brain development is completed by the age of thirteen; how that last 10 percent of the brain—the prefrontal cortex—takes another twelve years or so to fully develop.

She was fascinated to discover that the prefrontal cortex—that 10 percent of the brain that isn't fully developed until around age twenty-five—regulates decision-making skills and impulse control.

"Teens are getting cell phones at the age of thirteen or fourteen,"

Trisha loved computers and coding; but growing up, her heart really belonged to books. She especially loved *Where the Red Fern Grows* and the Great Brain books.

says Trisha. *"They're getting on social media, and they've been given this incredible responsibility online. And how ironic is it that they're not equipped to make good decisions?"*

She adds: *"Perhaps more importantly, quick, spur-of-the-moment, emotion-based decisions are really what drive them."*

And that was her "aha" moment. What if she could give teenagers a second chance to rethink their decisions—to rethink what they were sending—and how it might have an impact on the person on the receiving end?

So she designed and developed the ReThink alert—first as a browser extension, then as an app. If a potentially hurtful message is typed, an alert pops up, such as "Would you like to reword this?"

The user can hit "clear"—in which case the alert disappears, and they can send their message as is—or they can hit "OK" and rewrite their message however they see fit.

"Each word you type in is being plugged into the program— the algorithm—and if it hits a combination that is viewed as offensive, this app picks up on it, then flashes a ReThink alert,"

explains Trisha. "It can be difficult, because we don't want the app to pop up if you post something like 'I hate this weather.'"

In the development and experimentation phase, Trisha ran 1,500 trials with volunteer teenagers. In the analysis, she found that when adolescents received a second chance to rethink their decision, an astounding 93 percent of the time, they changed their minds.

Trisha and her ReThink app have had some fairly high-profile exposure: they were featured in a 2015 Super Bowl campaign to make the Internet safer, and she showcased the app at the White House Science Fair for President Obama.

Trisha pitched ReThink to the "sharks" on the hit show *Shark Tank,* and made a deal with two of them, who invested both money and expertise to help guide the product's growth. ReThink has received countless accolades, including being named one of the most innovative apps on Google Play. ReThink is now being used in thousands of schools on several different continents—and an antibullying ReThink movement is currently underway.

Trisha has received positive feedback from around the world: from teachers, parents, counselors, law enforcement, and most gratifyingly, from kids themselves.

"I've heard so many times, 'Yeah, I've posted something I regret-ted later, and maybe if I'd had the app I'd have thought through it a bit more—then I wouldn't end up being in a situation that I didn't need to be in.'"

Messaging friends via text, IM, and social media is what adolescents and teens do.

Ping: "What a loser!"

Ping: "You're such a moron!"

ReThink! Are those words really you?

With a pause to reconsider, more often than not, the answer is no.

MARGARET E. KNIGHT
Paper Bag Folding Machine

They're used every minute of every hour of every day by millions of people in thousands of stores across the United States and throughout the world. When she invented a machine that made flat-bottomed paper bags, Margaret E. Knight not only revolutionized the paper bag industry, but forever changed the way people shopped. No longer did they have to pack their milk, meats, and cheeses into heavy wooden crates. No longer did shoppers struggle to stuff jam and bread into bags shaped like envelopes. With the flat-bottomed paper bag, life suddenly got a whole lot easier.

Margaret's job at the Columbia Paper Bag Company was relatively simple. She needed to gather, stack, and tie the company's finished bags into neat bundles. Regular bags were made by machine; flat-bottomed bags by hand. She had been at work barely a week before the idea came to her.

"I had plenty of leisure time for making observations," Margaret said. "And such time was employed in watching the movement of the machines and the manufacture of square-bottomed bags by hand."

Why did flat-bottomed bags have to be made by hand? she wondered. It was time-consuming and very costly. Few customers could afford them. Margaret was told there was no such thing as a machine that could fold and paste flat bottoms. This seemed odd to her since the flat-bottomed kind was clearly the better bag.

Margaret had no formal training in engineering, but she had been working with or around machines— in cotton mills and manufacturing plants—from her earliest memory. In fact, as a child, she much preferred a jack-

"I've been to work all this evening trying the clockwork arrangement for making the square bottoms," Margaret wrote in her diary on Saturday, March 9, 1867. "It works well, so far so good. Have done enough for one day. If other parts work as well I shall be satisfied."

United States Patent Office.

MARGARET E. KNIGHT, OF BOSTON, MASSACHUSETTS.

Letters Patent No. 109,224, dated November 15, 1870.

IMPROVEMENT IN PAPER-FEEDING MACHINES.

No. 109,224.

Fig. 2.

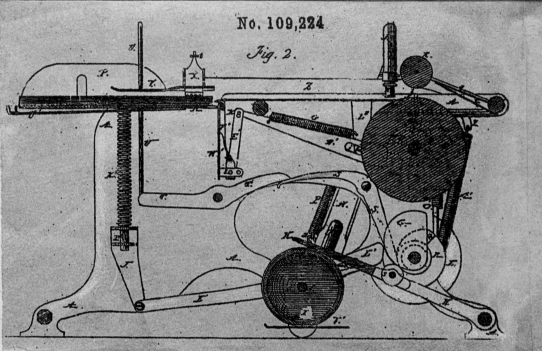

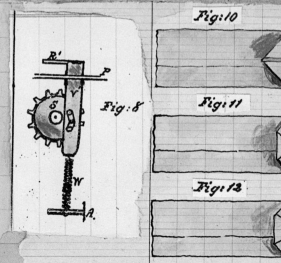

Fig: 8

Fig: 10

Fig: 11

Fig: 12

March 9, 1867

I've been to work all this evening trying the clockwork arrangement for making the square bottoms. It works well, so far so good. Have done enough for one day.

...upon the paper until the cockle is made, and rises away from it to release the upper sheet at the instant when it is taken hold of by the feed-mechanism to be drawn forward toward the cylinder.

knife, gimlet, and pieces of wood to dolls and other such toys.

She began by making drawings of her ideas. Next, she constructed a cutting tool that she called a guide finger, and created a folding tool from a piece of tin that she called a plate-knife folder. The result? A successfully folded square-bottomed bag.

"My next experiment was on one of my machines in the shop, to which I rigged these same two devices, my guide finger and plate-knife folder," she explained. *"By this means the paper tube followed along the guide finger entering it and flushing it back over the plate-knife folder. I did succeed in folding square bottoms."*

Once she established that a machine could, in fact, fold and paste square bottoms, Margaret was more determined than ever. A year after her initial idea, she successfully built a wooden model, about two and a half feet in length and one foot wide.

"In July of 1868, I then completed making it a perfect working model," stated Margaret. *"I should say that I made thousands of bags from it."*

She then hired a skilled machinist to build an iron version, which she needed to submit along with her patent application. Unfortunately, and unknown to Margaret, a man named Charles Annan saw her machine in the shop while it was being cast in iron. He copied it and tried to patent it as his own.

Determined to set the record straight, Margaret went to Washington, D.C., with her diary, patterns, photos, records, models, folded bags, witnesses, and her lawyer in tow to fight Annan's claims before the commissioner of patents.

After sixteen days of testimony, she won. The invention of the machine that makes flat-bottomed paper bags was acknowledged as Margaret Knight's and she was awarded a patent in 1870. She joined forces with a business partner and established the Eastern Paper Bag Company in Hartford, Connecticut, to manufacture her machines. She also set up a lab where

Although Margaret's invention has stood the test of time, she didn't get rich. Reportedly, she was offered $50,000 for her machine—the equivalent of more than half a million dollars today—but turned it down. It was noteworthy, then, that at her death her estate was worth a mere $275.05.

she worked on other inventions—amassing a total of twenty-seven patents—and prompting the media of the time to dub her "Lady Edison."

Margaret Knight's paper bag folding machine remains a milestone in the history of mechanical engineering. It's remarkable that during this era of high-tech gadgetry, a simple paper bag has remained a staple of everyday life. So, shoppers, toss some more chips and salsa into your cart. Your bag will hold them.

DR. PATRICIA BATH
Laserphaco Probe

Our eyes are windows to the world. But what happens when those windows get foggy? When faces of friends and words on a page and beautiful scenery become blurry, hazy, and yellow-tinged?

Enter Dr. Patricia Bath, whose invention of the Laserphaco Probe was a revolutionary new way to get rid of the fog—by removing cataracts. Cataracts are an all-too-common medical condition—typically affecting elderly people—whereby the lens of the eye changes from clear to cloudy, and a person's vision becomes foggy, blurred, and impaired.

That's certainly bad enough, but left untreated, cataracts will progressively worsen, causing blindness. Dr. Bath's invention has been credited with improving and saving the vision of thousands and thousands of suffering patients.

"I think in general I wanted to solve the tough problems—I wanted to take on the challenges," says Dr. Bath. "And at that time, the laser had never been dreamed of to remove the whole cataract— which is what my invention did."

As with many inventions, the idea for the Laserphaco Probe came about while Dr. Bath was struggling to solve a *different* ophthalmological problem (one that revolved around a surgical device used to get through scar tissue).

Dr. Patricia Bath is the first female African American doctor to receive a patent on a medical device.

Inspired by a conference presentation on surgical laser use, Dr. Bath had an "aha" moment regarding her scar tissue problem: if only she could transmit the laser energy (beam of light) through an optical fiber, the tiny fiber could then be safely inserted in the eye to cut away scar tissue.

And then . . . she made a crucial "what if" leap: if the laser was already in the eye, why not take out the entire cataract (the clouded eye lens) in one fell swoop? (As opposed to the methods available at the time, which required multiple steps and multiple incisions.) Once the cataract is removed, an artificial lens is placed in the eye to restore clear vision.

"The idea of transmitting the laser through a fiber, and then putting the fiber inside the eye . . . that had not been invented, and that was what my invention was," explains Dr. Bath.

In 1986, Dr. Bath took a sabbatical and devoted an extended period of time to exclusively research and experiment. Her experiments would require use of the powerful Excimer laser— nicknamed the Star Wars laser (named so because of the movie, and also because of then President Reagan's proposed missile laser defense system—which the press had dubbed "Star Wars").

Alas, the Star Wars laser wasn't available to scientists in America because the government had deemed it military grade, to be used for military operations only.

So she went to Berlin, where she was granted special permission to experiment with their Star Wars laser. She toiled with all the preliminary mathematics of the experiment, the parameters of the experiment, the intensity and the frequency of laser energy needed, the particular energy metric to be used,

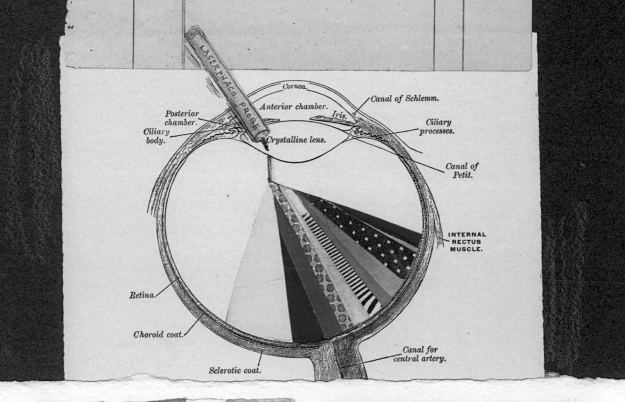

LASER PHACo. PROBE

Cornea.

Anterior chamber.

Canal of Schlemm.

Posterior chamber.

Iris.

Ciliary body.

Ciliary processes.

Crystalline lens.

Canal of Petit.

INTERNAL RECTUS MUSCLE.

Retina.

Choroid coat.

Sclerotic coat.

Canal for central artery.

as well as many other calculations and preparations (all necessary so the powerful laser wouldn't cause an explosion!).

"*You have to do all of that preliminary work before you can have the fun of actually executing it,*" she says. "*It was challenging, but when everything worked, it was a magical, eureka moment.*"

Dr. Bath succeeded in using a laser fiber, combined with an irrigation-aspiration device to create the Laserphaco Probe—which allowed for a single, small incision on the eye, and the removal of the full cataract.

"*The hardest part isn't coming up with the idea—that might be the easiest part,*" explains Dr. Bath, "*especially if you have a curious, inquisitive, or brilliant mind. But then translating the idea into reality . . . that's the tough part.*"

Dr. Bath knew when she presented her invention to the world at a scientific convention, it was going to be a big deal. So she flew her mom to the convention without telling her why. It was an enormously rewarding moment not only to hear oohs and aahs from the large audience but also to see how proud her mom was of her achievement.

She adds an important note: medical devices and methods continue to advance with time and with the advent of new technologies. And while the Laserphaco Probe was the cutting-edge tool for cataract removal in the 1990s, it has since been surpassed by new technology. Such is the nature of the medical field—and actually of inventions in general.

But years ago, an innovative woman created a tool to more efficiently, and less painfully, clean out the eye-fog. And with their windows to the world newly opened, people who once suffered from cataracts could once again see the faces of friends and words on the page and beautiful scenery—as crisp and clear as ever.

JEANNE LEE CREWS
Space Bumper

Jeanne plopped a chunk of metal—deformed by a deep crater—on her manager's desk. "We absolutely must do something!" she declared. She was referring to the problem of orbital debris in space—stuff like rocks, sand, and bits of metal that can crash into a satellite, shuttle, or space station. She had the prop to prove the devastating effects of a collision: destroyed space vehicles, destroyed experiments, destroyed lives.

"It's unbelievable the damage that can be done by things going at that speed," explains Jeanne. "I really cared about this problem—it

was a safety thing—so I persisted and became a real pain."

Finally, Jeanne Lee Crews, an aerospace engineer at NASA's Johnson Space Center, was given the green light to tackle the problem. Her goal was to find a lightweight shield that could withstand the extreme elements of space and protect the craft from debris—a space bumper of sorts. Her ingenuity sparked the development of several space shields—inventions that the space program could no longer safely function without.

Space debris travels at a speed of eighteen thousand miles per hour. That's three hundred miles per minute, and five miles per second. If you could travel at that speed, you could get to a store two and a half miles away—and back home—in one second.

The first part of the problem—coming up with the concept—was the easy part. Instead of using one thick shield of aluminum, the most commonly used shield, Jeanne would create a space bumper made of multiple layers. The next step was her toughest challenge: determining what materials to use and how to assemble them effectively. Jeanne came up with a creative solution: a ceramic fabric commonly used to line furnaces.

"We took this Nextel ceramic fabric and put it in a bunch of thin

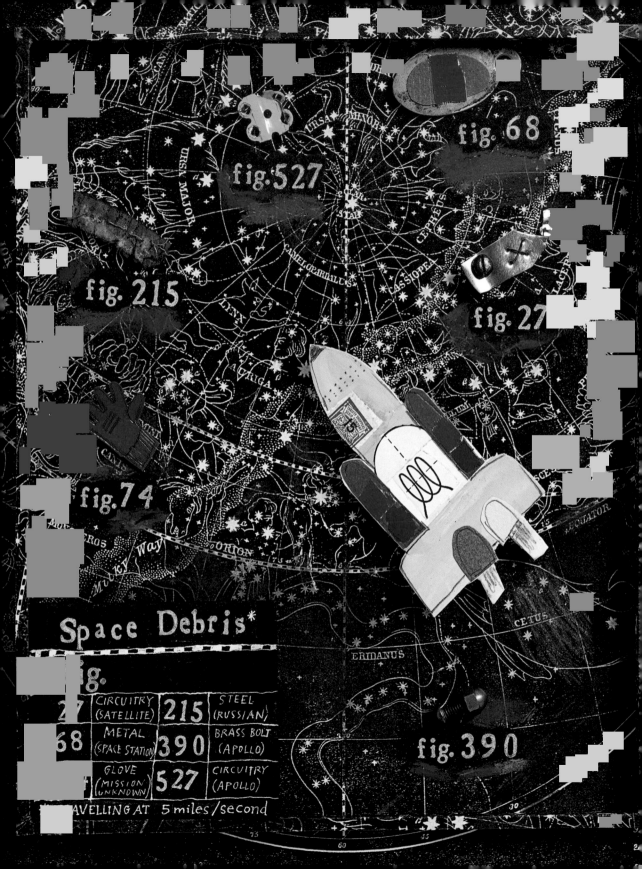

fig. 68

fig. 527

fig. 215

fig. 27

fig. 74

Space Debris*

fig.

27	CIRCUITRY (SATELLITE)	215	STEEL (RUSSIAN)
68	METAL (SPACE STATION)	390	BRASS BOLT (APOLLO)
	GLOVE (MISSION UNKNOWN)	527	CIRCUITRY (APOLLO)

TRAVELLING AT 5 miles/second

fig. 390

layers and created a flexible shield that had a really powerful shocker effect," Jeanne explains. "It shocks a particle once and then again and again and again."

Shocking a particle (creating shock waves on impact) causes it to become fragmented, or break apart. After designing and constructing the shield, Jeanne tested it for performance and workability. Of course, she couldn't test it in space, but there was another option. In a 150-foot-long metal building, Jeanne's team experimented. They simulated the conditions of a crash in space by using a high-tech tool called a light-gas gun.

"The biggest gun is about a hundred feet long, and we have a very high speed camera that goes a million frames per second," Jeanne says. "We take x-rays of the bullet while it's in flight. The guns are actually very simple. It's the diagnostics—making it all work together—that is the difficult part."

Months later, Jeanne successfully created the multishock shield, a combination of four layers of the ceramic fabric with three inches of air space in between. The total weight? Less than one sheet of aluminum. But now she had a new problem: designing a shield for the crew modules—the astronauts' living quarters—on the International Space Station. The modules had only four and a half inches of room for a shield, so the foot-thick multishock couldn't be used. Ever inventive, Jeanne and her coworkers simply modified the multishock shield—compressing it, or flattening it, and adding a new material. Maybe you've heard of it? . . . Kevlar.

Jeanne explains how the shield works: "First there's a piece of aluminum outside the spacecraft that breaks up the debris. A particle busts through that, gets broken up some, and hits the Nextel ceramic and then gets broken up a whole bunch."

Now, she said, there are still moving pieces that have tremendous energy—but they are slowed down considerably; to about the speed of a bullet, or one kilometer per second.

"So the Kevlar's behind the ceramic fabric and it slows it down again—so nothing gets to the back sheet," she says. "And that's the shield we're using on the space station."

The shields invented by Jeanne Crews and her coworkers are patented and belong to their employer, NASA. They are shields that will protect the astronauts, the space station, and critical experiments— experiments that are best carried out in the ideal conditions offered in space: particularly that of microgravity

(which is as close to zero gravity as we can come). Already, as a result of the knowledge gained through experimentation and exploration in space, we are able to enjoy hundreds of exciting products and reap the benefits of significant scientific advancements, including heart-rate monitors, diabetic pumps, bike helmets, and satellite TV. And who knows what else might be discovered in space? Maybe a nifty high-tech tennis racket, or perhaps a promising cure for cancer.

KIARA NIRGHIN
Combating Drought with Orange Peels

Orange peels and avocado skins: sliced, diced, and dried in the sun. Tasty? Perhaps not, but to bone-dry crops, it just might be the perfect recipe to quench their thirst—the perfect recipe for their very survival.

The media has dubbed her "the Girl Who Fights Drought with Fruit"—a snappy way to convey the essence of a ground-breaking scientific innovation created by Kiara Nirghin. Kiara invented a low-cost, biodegradable SAP, or superabsorbent polymer (made from orange peels and avocado skins), that might someday revolutionize how severe drought is battled. She was searching for a problem to tackle for the Google Science Fair competition, but Kiara really didn't have to look far.

The papers in her hometown of Johannesburg blasted the ominous national news day after day after day: "South Africa Experiencing Its Worst Drought in Thirty Years." "Crop Production in South Africa Severely Strained Due to Drought." Suitable area for planting maize dropped by 30 percent. And animals were dying off too—15 percent of the nation's cattle so far have succumbed to the drought. The cost of food staples (such as maize) has exploded as concerns of food shortages loom.

Even though she was a teenager, even though she had zero experience in the field of agriculture, even though the sheer enormity of the problem was mind-boggling, she wasn't scared off.

"My parents are not involved in science," says Kiara. "But they always told me I had the ability. They said if you do the research and you have the passion, you can do anything."

So she set out to research. Looking at mostly online resources—but also using the library—Kiara gradually began to understand the fundamentals of fighting drought.

When there is insufficient rainfall (South Africa, for example, was averaging about 34 percent less rain annually than normal for the region), studies have shown that mixing an SAP with the soil substantially helps that soil retain water—which, of course, in turn fuels the growth and survival of crops. (SAPs absorb, and hold on to, hundreds of times their weight in liquid.)

SAPs were proven to work—but were extremely expensive and not biodegradable. The question, then, that Kiara posed was this: Would it be possible to invent a new, biodegradable SAP that would hold water and keep the soil moist—and still be very low-cost? She decided to find out.

"Basically the orange was the first thing I tried," explains Kiara. *"Because of the research I did, I learned that what characterizes an SAP is its polysaccharide bonds. Then I found out that orange peels contain over 63 percent polysaccharide. So it just made sense to start there."*

One of Kiara's biggest challenges was fairly practical—time management. She was a full-time student with full-time homework, and finding the time to handle the demands of such a labor-intensive project was definitely difficult.

She describes much of her experimentation process as trial and error. Her first attempt, using orange peels alone, turned out not to

"...if YOU DO THE RESEARCH AND YOU HAVE THE PASSION, YOU CAN DO ANYTHING. **"**

13

work. Additional research led her to the concept of using oils, and Kiara thought the natural oils found in avocado skins might work nicely.

Kiara ran three experiments with six different SAPs—three commercially available ones (pectin, acrylic, and starch), and three orange peel variations that she had created: "orange peel solution," "orange peel powder," and "orange peel mixture."

"The first experiment I did was to calculate how much water each of the SAPs could retain," explains Kiara. "Next, I mixed the SAPs with topsoil and then saturated the soil with water—but only on the first day. [The experiment ran for twenty-one days.] For the last experiment, I attempted a real-life situation to see what effect the SAPs would have on a growing plant."

Her "orange peel mixture" outperformed the best of the commercial (acrylic) SAPs by retaining more water in the soil and getting better growth from the plant (in terms of height and flowering). And

Kiara entered the 2016 Google Science Fair with her Orange Peel SAP, and despite intense competition from around the world, she was awarded the grand prize! She was assigned a mentor to work with and try to develop the product for market. She also received a $50,000 educational scholarship!

the very best part? The top-performing "orange peel mixture" is also cheap. The acrylic SAP sells for roughly $3,000 per metric ton. The "orange peel mixture" would sell for about $60 a ton and could be made out of waste products from the juice manufacturing industry.

"Not much research had been done in the area I was interested in," says Kiara. "That was really the springboard for my idea: nobody else seemed to have thought of it."

The Girl Who Fights Drought with Fruit. Sounds like a new superhero—coming soon to a theater near you. And, in fact, if Kiara's SAP invention is commercially produced and used successfully in agriculture—there is no question, a new superhero will have been born.

PATSY O. SHERMAN
Scotchgard

It's a party: lots of people, lots of laughs, lots of food. Ten unwrapped presents, six spilled sodas, three dropped cup-cakes, and two slopped sandwiches later, the party is over. The guests are gone, and the mess is left behind. A stained sofa? A spotted rug? Maybe not.

Spills happen. Sometimes you just wipe up your juice, toss the towel in the sink, and head outside to play soccer. Other times you invent a product that forever changes the textile industry. That's exactly what Patsy O. Sherman did when she invented Scotchgard fabric protector. Hired as a scientist by the 3M laboratories in 1952 on a temporary project, she was supposed to create a new type of fuel hosing to be used on jet aircrafts. One day, while Patsy was making a rubbery synthetic latex mixture, there was an accident.

"A little brown, four-ounce bottle of this sticky latex mixture was dropped on the floor," Patsy explained. *"It broke—splashed all over the assistant's canvas tennis shoes."*

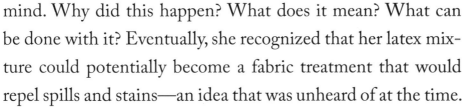

They tried to clean the white shoes; tried water, tried soap. They used every cleaning solution in the lab, but the spill resisted all attempts. As she noticed the cleaning materials bead up on the splotch, several questions ran through Patsy's mind. Why did this happen? What does it mean? What can be done with it? Eventually, she recognized that her latex mixture could potentially become a fabric treatment that would repel spills and stains—an idea that was unheard of at the time.

The actual blob that spilled on the shoe was never ideal for fabric—it was much too sticky, too gummy. Patsy and her co-inventor, Sam Smith, had to design and create products specifically for use on fabric. Their initial attempts were rather disastrous.

"The first time the product was too sticky. They ran the fabric through the mill and it caused this sticky rubber to build up on the

Scotchgard | No Scotchgard

29

Scotchgard | No Scotchgard

35

Scotchgard | No Scotchgard

37

Scotchgard | No Scotchgard

48

Scotchgard | No Scotchgard

56

Scotchgard | No Scotchgard

68

TOMATO SOUP
2 9

CRAYON
3 5

COFFEE
3 7

PAINT
4 8

INK
5 6

GRAPE JUICE
6 8

SODA POP
10 6

RASPBERRY JAM
1 2 4

Scotchgard | No Scotchgard

106

Scotchgard | No Scotchgard

124

squeeze rolls," recalled Patsy. "The next product we made was a little too hard and too brittle, and when that went through the squeeze rolls it got all hard and powdery."

During this experimentation phase, Patsy waited for word of her product's performance. Believe it or not, she couldn't supervise the process because she wasn't even allowed in the textile mills simply because she was a woman! In the 1950s, discrimination against women was widespread not only in the textile mills, but also in the general workplace. A lot of men assumed that women didn't have the skills or abilities necessary to succeed in business and feared that women would just "get in the way."

Patsy received several patents for her fabric protectors, and 3M marketed them under the trademark Scotchgard. Although she didn't receive any money for her inventions, her temporary job became a permanent one—and lasted forty years.

"It took a while to get a product to meet the needs of the consumer," said Patsy. "Then we had to learn to prepare it in an economical fashion so the consumer would be willing to pay for it."

After the introduction of Scotchgard in 1956, Patsy spent the next several years improving the product and creating new variations for specific uses and fabrics. She points out that other 3M scientists also became involved in the development of Scotchgard and some of them made very important discoveries.

But her biggest challenge was yet to come—developing a protector for the new permanent-press fabrics. Because of the nature of the permanent-press fabric, Patsy needed to find something that would both repel stains and release them once the fabric was washed. Impossible, people said. Patsy wasn't so sure. Her first experiments yielded exciting results. The very next day the project had grown so big that every person in the lab was working on it.

When the affordable, permanent-press Scotchgard was created, the manager of the manufacturing plant sent a note to 3M stating that they had mixed a large batch of the product and now had a year's supply. A few days later, the entire stock was sold.

"We suddenly had one that everyone wanted to buy," she recalled. *"And that was when the product took off."*

Thanks to an accidental spill and the inventiveness of Patsy Sherman and her colleagues, everyday spills are no longer a problem. Today, there are more than one hundred kinds of Scotchgard protectors and cleaners—although the original concoction has been reformulated to reflect the needs of today's market, as well as to remove chemicals that were later found to be harmful. The products are sold in more than fifty countries around the world and have made the 3M company millions and millions of dollars. Chances are, most new furniture and carpets are pretreated with a fabric protector at the factory. So go ahead and spill your soup or slop your pop. Just be sure to clean it up.

Nine years before her invention of Scotchgard, Patsy took a general-interest test in high school. In 1947, girls and boys took separate tests. Despite the fact that she wanted to be a scientist, her test indicated that she was well suited to be a housewife. Unsatisfied, she demanded to take the boys' test. The results? A career in dentistry or chemistry.

ANN MOORE
Snugli

There was always so much to do: work at the computer, work in the yard, go to the store, make lunch, clean up lunch—and all the while keep the baby calm and content. Parents and babysitters everywhere have struggled to hold and comfort their baby while attending to other tasks. What we need, they joked, are more hands. What they got was better.

It began in West Africa with a two-year tour of duty in the Peace Corps. As a pediatric nurse, Ann Moore had plenty of opportunities to observe babies, their mothers, and the closeness they shared. The African babies were always cradled in bright cloth wraps and slung on their mothers' back, and Ann noticed that they seemed very secure and content. Back home, with the birth of her own baby, Ann was determined to recreate the comfort and convenience of the African carrier. And that's exactly what she did. Along the way, her creation just happened to spark a multimillion-dollar business: the Snugli baby pouch.

"I tried the African method," Ann explained. "It's just a piece of fabric about three yards long. They balance the baby on their back and then tie this long piece of fabric around their chest and waist. I could never make that stay," said Ann, laughing. "After a little while, the baby would always slide down my back, and I felt very insecure with that."

So Ann turned to her mother, Lucy Aukerman, for help. Using photos from the African trip as a model, Ann's mom fashioned a cloth baby carrier that was more functional and easier to wear. The carrier was a cozy pouch with two holes for the baby's legs and shoulder straps to fasten it to Ann's back.

"We had no thought of ever marketing it," recalled Ann. "It was just for me to have my hands free and have a happy baby."

It worked wonderfully. Everywhere Ann went, people commented on her ingenious baby carrier. "Where can I get one?" they would ask.

"So my mother would make one for them, and I'd send it off,"

explained Ann. "That's how it all started and how it grew really—just by word of mouth."

It was 1965, and Ann and her mother were selling two baby carriers a month. When their carrier was mentioned in the *Whole Earth Catalogue,* sales instantly jumped to eighteen a month. Now it was time to get serious. Ann, her mother, and her husband, Mike, brainstormed for a name.

The packaging of Snuglis was done in a long, cinderblock building—a converted dog kennel. And the handmade versions were created in a production facility on Ann's parents' farm—in a converted chicken house.

Mike quit his job to work on marketing the Snugli full-time. They applied for a patent and formed a company. They designed special packaging and made minor improvements.

"The first one did not have adjustable shoulder straps," said Ann. "I hadn't realized that I had to get it over coats and thicker things. So then we had to figure out a way to make it adjustable."

The demand for Snuglis continued to grow. By the early 1970s, Ann's company was hand-making and selling three hundred carriers a month. And then . . .

"In 1975, Consumer Reports *did a little review of baby carriers and they said the Snugli was the best," explained Ann.*

Over the years, Ann has received several photos from zookeepers carrying baby animals. It seems that some zoo animals—including baby chimps and baby kangaroos—find the Snugli cozy and comfortable too.

Then the company really took off. By 1979, they had designed a new version of the Snugli—with a stiffer fabric that could be reproduced in a factory. They still sold the handmade versions, but the factory-made ones offered customers a less costly alternative. Now the Snugli company was making *8,000* carriers by hand and 25,000 in the factory every month. By 1984, yearly sales had reached $6 million. After several different offers, Ann and Mike finally sold the company in 1985 to the Huffy Corporation. And for moms and pops and babies on the go, Ann Moore's Snugli has become a necessity, a must-have, a what-in-the-world-would-we-do-without-it sort of product. In short, who needs more hands?

ALICE BROOKS AND BETTINA CHEN
Roominate

Dream it. Design it. Build it. Wire up the lights, wire up the motors to the fans, machines, and elevators. Build the circuits, re-check the connections. Sounds like a job for an engineer. And it is. Or . . . for an eight-year-old who's in a problem-solving mood, feeling creative, and looking for fun.

In an effort to expose more girls to engineering, Alice Brooks and Bettina Chen invented Roominate—a toy modular building set complete with do-it-yourself electrical circuits that can power tiny lights and motors.

Alice and Bettina were grad students in engineering, and they recall being caught completely off-guard by how few women were in their classes. They thought it was a big problem and wondered what, if anything, they could do to help inspire girls to choose engineering fields.

"When we were growing up," says Alice, *"we both had experiences with engineering and with inventing things—particularly outside of school, which made it fun."*

Bettina recalls building and constructing with Legos a lot while growing up. Alice remembers once asking for a doll for her birthday and being given a saw instead. She then used her saw and made herself a doll from wood.

While in college, they both attributed their confidence and comfort in physics and math and with hands-on spatial learning to their early exposure with engineering basics.

"We talked about this," recalls Alice, *"and I think that was our 'light bulb moment' . . . that we should start out with play—and take it completely outside of the classroom. That's how we can hook them in."*

Their very first product attempt actually was a modular

building toy, but they decided it wasn't very good, so they moved on to their next idea. They tried little cars with motors you put in yourself, but when they watched kids play, the kids weren't that engaged. Next, they experimented with transforming the cars into pets, but that also fell flat.

"I think the important thing was," says Alice, *"we kept putting something out there and we kept trying to make it more engaging and more appealing."*

After several failed attempts, they regrouped and asked themselves: What are we trying to do? What are we trying to accomplish? The answer was surprisingly straightforward: they wanted to get kids—especially girls—interested in building and using circuits.

So they brainstormed different trends they had seen, and recalled seeing a lot of dollhouses that just sat in the corner—familiar and comfortable to play with, but not really challenging or expanding any play boundaries. That's when the idea struck: give kids a set of materials to build and wire little rooms, which they could then play with.

The first set they debuted was anything but fancy: pieces of foam core, craft paper, Popsicle sticks, and little motors ripped out of cars from their previous trial.

"The difference in engagement was just amazing!" recalls Alice. *"We were in a room with about twenty kids and they were literally*

saying to their parents, 'I'm not done, Mom. Let me keep playing!'
Then they'd turn to me and say, 'I need more circuits.' That's when
we knew we had the seed of an idea that could really take off."

From there, it was a process of iterating and testing it out
with kids. They brought it to Maker Faire in 2012, where hundreds of kids visited their booth—and conveyed to Alice and
Bettina that it still wasn't modular
enough. The kids wanted even
more freedom and options
and pieces to create their
own designs.

Soon they were ready
to test its marketability
and raise money for pro-
duction costs. They started
a crowdfunding Kickstarter
campaign—raising their goal of
$25,000 in just six days.

> After Kickstarter, they enlisted some of their friends to help pack and ship their first orders. They threw a football party in their warehouse—projecting the game up on the wall—and they all worked to put together 2,000 orders.

Two years after they launched Roominate, Alice and Bettina pitched the product to the "sharks" on *Shark Tank*—hoping for an investment to grow the company. They got one—along
with a uniquely structured deal from the investing "shark" to
allow his two young daughters to hang out at the company and
learn how to turn an innovative idea into a successful business.

"There were tons of challenges along the way," says Alice. "But it's been so rewarding seeing how our products are used, and the creative things the girls come up with—and how proud they are of their creations!"

Kids have built houses with working fans and working elevators. They've built beds, desks, tables, and chairs. They've built bridges that light up, working carousels, cars, and airplanes. Roominate continues to develop its products—offering more pieces and more circuits—reflecting the kids' boundless creativity.

It will take a few years yet to know whether or not playing with the toy inspired any girls to pursue degrees in engineering; but in the meantime, kids will continue to dream it, design it, build it, and wire it all up . . . simply because it's fun.

YOUR TURN

Suppose you have an invention of your own. It's different, it's new, it's neat. Now what? Obtaining a patent may be an important first step. A patent is the legal document issued by the government to protect an idea. Utility patents are for inventions that are either mechanical or electrical in nature. Design patents cover inventions that are new, as well as original designs of existing products.

To patent an invention, you must prove that it is new and useful and that you are the very first person to have invented the item. A patent application must be complete with diagrams, notes, and models. If your invention proves to be unique, you pay the fees and are assigned a patent number. Your invention is then legally protected for twenty years (from the date of filing for a utility patent), and you alone have the right to profit from it.

Not all inventions, however, will benefit from having a patent. The patent process can be extremely expensive and, depending on the invention, might not be really necessary. A good patent attorney should be able to advise you on the merits of obtaining a patent for your specific invention.

For more information on the patent process:

U.S. Patent and Trademark Office
uspto.gov
Inventors Assistance Center (IAC)
(800) 786-9199

There are several contests and organizations that encourage young people to innovate. The following is a small sample of what's available.

National Inventors Hall of Fame
    invent.org
    Camp Invention: campinvention@invent.org

Young Scientist Challenge
    Discovery/3M
    youngscientistlab.com

Google Science Fair
    googlesciencefair.com

Intel International Science and Engineering Fair
    student.societyforscience.org

Young Inventors' Program (YIP)
    Invention Convention
    aas-world.org

United Inventors Association of America (UIA)
    uiausa.org

International Federation of Inventors' Association (IFIA)
    ifia.com

Maker Faire
    makerfaire.com

Select Sources

Al-Ardah, Nour. Email correspondence with the author. Eden Prairie, MN, 2017.

Associated Press. "Palestinian Girls Get Ticket to Intel Science Fair." April 27, 2010, Arab News.

Bath, Dr. Patricia. Interview by author. Audio recording (telephone). Eden Prairie, MN, 2017.

Billings, Charlene W. *Grace Hopper: Navy Admiral and Computer Pioneer.* Hillside, NJ: Enslow, 1989.

Born Just Right. www.bornjustright.org

Brooks, Alice. Interview by author. Audio recording (telephone). Eden Prairie, MN, 2017.

Burgess, Kim. "Young Inventor Creates App to Save Kids Left in Hot Cars." *Albuquerque Journal,* January 2, 2017.

Chavez, Alissa. Interview by author. Audio recording (telephone). Eden Prairie, MN, 2017.

Crews, Jeanne Lee. Interview by author. Audio recording (telephone). Minneapolis, February 10, 1998.

Dewedar, Rasha. "Student Finds New Way of Turning Plastic into Biofuel." *SciDev.Net,* June 29, 2012.

The Empowerment Plan. www.empowermentplan.org/the-coat.

Faiad, Azza Abdelhamid. Interview by author. Audio recording (telephone). Eden Prairie, MN, 2017.

Freeman, Chris. "Roominate Update After Shark Tank—How They're Doing in 2017." *Gazette Review,* April 15, 2016.

Global Women Inventors and Innovators Network. www.gwiin.com.

Google Science Fair. www.googlesciencefair.com/en.

Hamacher, Adriana, and Andra Keay. "Twenty-Five Women in Robotics You Need to Know About—2015." *Robohub,* October 13, 2015.

Karnes, Frances A., Ph.D., and Suzanne M. Bean, Ph.D. *Girls and Young Women Inventing.* Minneapolis: Free Spirit Publishing, 1995.

Kwolek, Stephanie. Interview by author. Audio recording (telephone). Minneapolis, January 20, 1998.

Lee, J. A. N. "Unforgettable Grace Hopper." *Reader's Digest,* October 1994, pp. 181–85.

Lemelson Center for the Study of Invention and Innovation. www.invention.si.edu.

LuminAID. www.luminaid.com

Ma'an News Agency. "Palestinian Girls Win Award for Sensor Cane at Intel Fair." May 18, 2010.

Macdonald, Anne L. *Feminine Ingenuity: Women and Invention in America.* New York: Ballantine, 1992.

McKeown, Blanche. "She Invented the Windshield Wiper." *Record,* January 1956, pp. 10–12.

Monks, Kieron. "Sixteen-Year-Old South African Invents Wonder Material to Fight Drought." *CNN,* August 14, 2016.

Moore, Ann. Interview by author. Audio recording (telephone). Minneapolis, June 17, 1998.

National Institutes of Health. "Changing the Face of Medicine." October 14, 2003. (Updated: June 10, 2013) cfmedicine.nlm.nih.gov.

National Inventors Hall of Fame. www.invent.org.

Nirghin, Kiara. Interview by author. Audio recording (telephone). Eden Prairie, MN, 2017.

Prabhu, Trisha. Interview by author. Audio recording (telephone). Eden Prairie, MN, 2017.

Reeves, Lynn. "Concern Gave Boon to Drivers." *Birmingham News,* February 13, 1972, pp. 10–12.

ReThink Words: www.rethinkwords.com/inthenews.

Showell, Ellen H., and Fred M. B. Amram. *From Indian Corn to Outer Space: Women Invent in America.* Peterborough, NH: Cobblestone Publishing, 1995.

Stallworth, Clarke. "Southern Belle Invented Wiper for Windshield." *Birmingham News,* February 20, 1977.

Stanley, Autumn. *Mothers and Daughters of Invention: Notes for a Revised History of Technology.* Metuchen, NJ: Scarecrow Press, 1993.

Stork, Anna. Interview by author. Audio recording (telephone). Eden Prairie, MN, 2017.

U.S. Patent and Trademark Office: Before the Commissioner of Patents. "Testimony for Margaret E. Knight; Deposition of Margaret E. Knight." Boston, May 5, 1870.

U.S. Patent and Trademark Office. "Specification forming part of Letters Patent No. 743,801," Mary Anderson, of Birmingham, Alabama, Window-Cleaning Device. November 10, 1903.

Vare, Ethlie Ann, and Greg Ptacek. *Mothers of Invention: From the Bra to the Bomb, Forgotten Women and their Unforgettable Ideas.* New York: William Morrow, 1988.

Vare, Ethlie Ann, and Greg Ptacek. *Women Inventors and Their Discoveries.* Minneapolis: Oliver Press, 1993.

Women Inventors Network. www.ifia.com/women-inventors.

Glossary

"aha" moment: a moment of sudden realization, inspiration, insight, recognition, or comprehension. Also called eureka or light bulb moment.

aspiration: drawing something in, out, up, or through, by, or as if by, suction.

biodegradable: capable of being broken down by the action of living things.

catalyst: a substance that enables a chemical reaction to proceed at a usually faster rate or under different conditions (as at a lower temperature) than otherwise possible.

circuit: an assemblage of electronic elements to create the complete path of an electric current includ-ing usually the source of electric energy.

counterweight: an equivalent weight or force.

crowdfunding: the practice of obtaining needed funding (as for a new business) by soliciting contributions from a large number of people especially from the online community.

curing (curing corn): to prepare or alter especially by chemical or physical processing for keeping or use.

entrepreneur: a person who starts a business and is willing to risk loss in order to make money.

gimlet: a small tool with a screw point, grooved shank, and cross handle for boring holes.

infrared: infrared light lies between the visible and microwave portions of the electromagnetic spectrum.

irrigation: the therapeutic flushing of a body part with a stream of liquid.

iterate/iterating: to do again and again.

LED: a semiconductor diode that emits light when a voltage is applied to it; used especially in electronic devices (as for an indicator light).

mentor: a trusted counselor or guide, tutor or coach.

modular: constructed with standardized units or dimensions for flexibility and variety.

multifaceted: having many different parts or aspects.

NGO: nongovernmental organization.

ophthalmological: relating to ophthalmology, the branch of medicine concerned with the study and treatment of diseases of the eye.

petroleum: an oily, flammable liquid that is refined into gas or other products.

polymer: a chemical compound consisting of repeating structural units.

polysaccharide bond: any of a class of carbohydrates formed by repeating units linked together by glycosidic bonds.

prosthestic: an artificial body part (prosthesis: device to replace or augment a missing or impaired part of the body).

prototype: a full-scale and usually functional form of a new type or design of a construction.

superabsorbent polymer (SAP): a material that can absorb and retain extremely large amounts of liquids relative to its own mass.

Acknowledgments

The author wishes to thank the following for their contributions:

Du Pont; Katherine Hagmeier, 3M; Roz O'Hearn, Nestlé; Ellen Walley, NASA; Carrie Ahlborn, Brewster Academy; Eunice McSweeney, Whitman Historical Commission; U.S. Patent and Trademark Office; Danielle Frizi, the Gillette Company; Stanley Bauman Photography; Herral Long Photography; Dr. Roger F. Murray II; A'Lelia Bundles/Madam Walker Family Collection; Charlene Billings; J. A. N. Lee; Ann Moore; Alexia Abernathy; Patsy Sherman; Stephanie Kwolek; Jeanne Crews; Rebecca Schroeder Perry; Valerie L. Thomas; Ty Sheppard, Google; Lindsay Yanek, QVC; Daphna Gall, LuminAID; Sarah Gumina, Roominate; Bhanu Prabhu; Trisha Prabhu; Kiara Nirghin; Rekha Nirghin; Alissa Chavez; Azza Abdelhamid Faiad; Anna Stork; Alice Brooks; Patricia Bath; Jordan and Jen Reeves; Nour Al-Ardah; the extraordinary Ann Rider; and the entire team at Houghton Mifflin Harcourt.

Index

1980s (cont.)

Cheryl Moore: *pressure-sensitive adhesives*

Connie Hubbard (and Ray Heyer): *Scotch-Brite Never Rust wool soap pads*

Jeanne Lee Crews: *space bumper*

Karla Sachi: *Space Kids 3000 dolls*

Estelle Panzer, Janis Odensky and Judy Jordan: *Tradition (board game: a Jewish version of Trivial Pursuit)*

Valerie L. Thomas: *illusion transmitter*

Mildred Smith: *The Family Treedition (board game)*

Martina Kempf: *voice-controlled wheelchair*

Lucy Hammett: *Texas Bingo (board game)*

Helen G. Gonet: *electronic Bible*

Frances Gabe: *self-cleaning house*

Dorothy Young Kirby: *Universal Stitching Guide*

Anne L. Macdonald: *method of hand-knitting a patterned fabric*

Laurene H. O'Donnell: *drinking fountain device and combination drinking fountain and sink device*

Penny Cooper: *flat food pouch*

Carolyn Davidson and Kathy Redfern: *You Said It (board game)*

Margaret Grimaldi: *space shuttle escape pole*

Katie Harding (five years old): *mud puddle spotter*

Lila Beauchamp: *antiviral compounds*

Janine Jagger: *retractable safety needle*

1990s

Naomi Nakao: *Nakao Snare (surgical retrieval assembly)*

Dr. Robin Murphy: *search and rescue robots*

Ann Tsukamoto: *process to isolate human stem cells*

Patty Billings: *Geobond*

Joy Mangano: *Miracle Mop (plus many other inventions)*

Lori Greiner: *jewelry organizer (plus many other inventions)*

Esther Sans Takeuchi: *Li/SVO battery*

Amy B. Smith: *phase-change incubator*

Misha Mahowald: *silicon eye*

Kerry and Shirley Worgan: *Baby Faces video*

Christine Hanisco: *hair accessories*

Cindy Huber and Nancy Longo: *HealthyBurgers (veggie burgers)*

Jen Laver: *Piddlers (toilet-training targets)*

Jane Malin: *Discrete Event Simulation Tool for Analysis of Qualitative Models of Continuous Processing Systems (for NASA)*

Stacey Crowell: *Beach Caddie*

Eve Abrams Wooldridge: *device to precisely measure space contamination*

Julie Austin: *HydroSport (lightweight water bottles attached to wrists)*

Georgena Terry: *bicycle saddle for women*

Jeanie Low (ten years old): *Kiddie Stool (it folds into a cabinet)*

Mary Ellen Hills: *Dazzle Dot (lipstick mirror)*

Hatice Cullingford: *Apparatus and Method for Cellulose Processing Using Microwave Pretreatment (recycling in space) for NASA*

Mary Putre: *"revenge toilet paper" (novelty gift)*

Vanessa Singer: *musical percussion product*

Alexia Abernathy: *Oops! Proof No-Spill Feeding Bowl*

Barbara Arnold: *Change-A-Robe, Handi-Robe*

Suzi Havens: *Havens portable training system (exercise equipment)*

2000s

Helen Greiner (co-inventor): *Roomba vacuum*

Cricket Lee: *Fitlogic (clothing standard)*

Robin Murphy: *search and rescue robots*

Maja Mataric: *socially assistive robots*

Cecilia Laschi: *biorobotics technologies*

Seema Prakash: *Glass Bead Liquid culture technology (cheap plant cloning)*

Bethlehem Tilahun Alemu: *soul rebel shoes*

Deborah Adler: *ClearRx prescription medication bottle/system (in partnership with Target)*

Maria del Socorro Flores Gonzalez: *diagnostic technique for invasive amebiasis*

Yuki Nakagawa (and team): *robot RIC90*

Lisa Becker: *Ostomysecrets (undergarments to conceal ostomy bag)*

Petra Wadstrom: *water treatment/solar water heater*

Mikaila Ulmer: *Me & the Bees lemonade*

Stephanie Boom: *Wondercide organic pet-care products*

Angela Cody-Rouget: *Major Mom home organization systems*

Remya Jose: *bicycle washing machine*

Sara Blakely: *Spanx*

Emily Cummins: *pull-able water carrier for manual workers*

Mandy Haberman: *Anywayup Cup, first completely spill-proof cup*

Omowunmi Sadik: *microelectrode biosensors*

Ileana Sanchez: *book for blind bringing art and Braille together*

2010 to Present

Anna Stork (co-inventor): *LuminAID lanterns*

Andrea Sreshta (co-inventor): *LuminAID lanterns*

Veronika Scott: *sleeping-bag coat for homeless*

Mai Lieu: *Crea products*

Azza Abdelhamid Faiad: *plastics to biofuel*

Angela Zhang: *nanoparticle cancer treatment*

Deepika Kurup: *water purification system*

Pree Walia (co-inventor): *Nailbot (nail-decorating robot)*

Stephanie Lacour: *robotics semiconductor devices that stretch and still retain electronic properties*